EDITING GUIDE

A HANDBOOK FOR WRITERS AND EDITORS

EDITING GUIDE

A HANDBOOK FOR WRITERS AND EDITORS

by RACHEL BARD

R & M PRESS · **Tacoma** · **Washington**

Library of Congress Catalog Card Number 89-92409

ISBN 0-929838-02-5

TABLE OF CONTENTS

EDITING GUIDE

A HANDBOOK FOR WRITERS AND EDITORS

PREFACE

For the purposes of this book, editing simply means improving what has been written, whether you wrote it or someone else did. Most writers and editors realize that almost any piece of writing will benefit from another look. This brief guide will point out what to look for, and what to do if changes are needed.

The book is organized in two sections. The first gives general guidelines for clear, concise, effective writing. The second lists and illustrates the most frequently encountered difficulties in style — including punctuation, spelling and grammar. Following this section you will find the editing and proofreading symbols that are universally used and understood by editors, printers and publishers.

There are a number of excellent texts on editing, as well as comprehensive manuals of style. Some of these are listed in the bibliography. Every writer and editor should be familiar with such books. This Editing Guide is not intended to replace them, but rather to provide quick answers to common questions.

For the experienced writer or editor, it will serve as a refresher and a useful handbook. For the beginner, it will introduce the basic rules for acceptable writing and the editing techniques needed to apply them.

By combining brevity with an easy-to-use format, it should save time for anybody who works with words.

Part I

Guidelines for Good Writing

Most writers and editors can benefit from a periodic reminder of what characterizes clear, readable, concise writing. The guidelines that follow are intended to refresh your memory of the precepts you have been familiar with since you first started working with words, and to strengthen your resolve to follow them.

1

BE BRIEF.

To quote the immortal William Strunk, "Omit needless words."

If you haven't read Rule No. 17 in "Elements of Style" lately, do so. It will remind you of the worth of concise, lean writing, inspire you to be more ruthless in cutting copy, and show you some words and phrases to watch for that could and probably should be taken out.

Not only will cutting the unnecessary words themselves shorten the sentence; you will often find that this also opens the way to rephrasing the whole sentence so that it says what it means in the clearest, briefest way possible.

Examples of words and phrases that could be omitted:

"the fact" as in "I was unaware (of the fact)
that the plane was two hours late."

Even better (shorter): "I did not know the plane was two hours late."

"who is" or "who was" as in "Thomas Jefferson, (who was) our third president, was as interested in natural history as he was in politics."

"which was" as in "The economic recovery, (which was) predicted by the Secretary, came to pass right on cue."

"the question as to" as in "The council then discussed (the question as to) whether a no-growth ordinance should be passed."

Even better: "The council then debated the no-growth ordinance."

"there is no doubt but that" as in "(There is no doubt but that) another cold snap is on the way."

"is a subject that" as in "Most people agree that this (is a subject that) deserves a full debate."

"the fact is" as in "(The fact is,) there is far less danger from wrong-headedness among the voters than there is from apathy."

As Strunk says: "If you feel you are possessed of the truth, or a fact, simply state it. Do not give it advance billing."

2

BE CLEAR.

Say what you mean. Don't make your reader guess, or stumble over awkward constructions. How can you catch the barriers to comprehension? One suggestion: let what you have written sit overnight. Then read it over, trying to put yourself in the place of a reader who has never seen it. Be alert for anything that could be misunderstood, or cause the reader to wonder what you mean.

These are things to watch for:

1. Sentences that are too long. Often, by simply making an unwieldy sentence into two shorter ones you will do the reader a favor.

Example:

> Providing round-the-clock information on a wide range of subject areas including science and technology, business, arts, entertainment, politics and law, as well as history and geography, this electronic encyclopedia is an invaluable source of current information, at your fingertips, without leaving your chair or opening a book.
>
> Better: Without leaving your chair or opening a book, you may access this invaluable electronic encyclopedia. It provides information around the clock, on a wide range of subjects, including science and technology...

2. Beginning with a long prepositional phrase. This may make the reader wait too long before finding out what you are trying to say; and may result in a cumbersome, wordy sentence.

Example:

> Besides his ashtray, favorite pen, glass of iced tea, notebook, photo of his dead wife, blotter, gold clock and dictionary, the writer's desk held — precisely in the center— his

most prized possession, the ancient Remington typewriter that had been his constant companion for 20 years.

Better: The writer's most prized possession, the ancient Remington typewriter that had been his constant companion for 20 years, sat precisely in the center of his desk. It was surrounded by his ashtray...

3. Misplaced modifiers. If the modifier is too far from the word it modifies, confusion may result.

Depending on the meaning, the sentence below could be corrected in either of two ways:

Example:

Wrong: The innovators of the Impressionist school, so scorned in the last century, are now accepted as Old Masters.

Better: The innovators of the Impressionist school, which was so scorned in the last century, are now accepted as Old Masters.

Or: The innovators of the Impressionist school, who were so scorned in the last century, are now accepted as Old Masters.

4. Awkward or illogical sentence construction, which can produce ambiguous or ridiculous misreadings.

Examples:

> Wrong: The general was complimented on his handling of the revolt by the President.
>
> Better: The general was complimented by the President on his handling of the revolt.
>
> Even better (active, not passive):The President complimented the general on his handling of the revolt.
>
> Wrong: The mayor announced he was planning a vacation in Florida while the council was out of the room.
>
> Better: While the council was out of the room, the mayor announced he was planning a vacation in Florida.

BE CONSISTENT.

Style rules are not universal. Authorities differ. What's all right with the AP "Stylebook" may be frowned on by the University of Chicago "Manual of Style." It is up to you, as a writer or editor, to decide which rules you will follow, and then to stick to your decision. In other words, be consistent, even if you're going against some accepted practice.

Consider the serial comma — that is, a comma before the conjunction that joins the last two items in a series. The "Manual of Style" recommends its use.

For example:

We have a choice of copper, silver, or gold.

BE CONSISTENT.

The "Stylebook" does not.

For example:

> We have a choice of copper, silver or gold.

(See discussion of the serial comma in the chapter on Punctuation in Part II.)

You need to choose which of the two practices you will adhere to, and then be consistent in your adherence.

The same thing applies to other variables. For example, spelling. Will you spell it judgment or judgement? The dictionary permits either. Most U.S. writers prefer judgment, while the British prefer judgement.

Or numbers. Some authorities spell out all numbers through 99; others (including the editors of this book) spell out all numbers through nine, and use figures from 10 on, with certain exceptions.

Or plurals of numerals, such as dates. The "Stylebook" recommends simply adding *s*.

For example:

> The weather was worse in the 1930s.

However, many dictionaries, and The New York Times, use *'s*:

> The music is reminiscent of the 1930's.

The important thing is to be consistent in your style. Make your own rules if you like, but don't break them.

If writing or editing a long manuscript, make yourself a style sheet: an alphabetical list of things to watch for, such as spelling of unfamiliar names or words, special treatment of punctuation, capitalization, use of hyphens, abbreviations, etc. You will find useful guidance on style sheets in Karen Judd's "Copyediting" and in the University of Chicago "Manual of Style."

USE THE RIGHT WORD.

Many words have been misused so much that they sound right. But your reader just might know the difference. Why take a chance? Especially when it's so easy to look it up.

In Strunk & White's "Elements of Style," see Chapter IV for a good discussion of misused words.

Listed below are 21 words that seem to cause the most trouble. You are advised to learn to use them correctly, in order to avoid offending at least some of your readers.

21 COMMONLY MISUSED WORDS

adverse, averse

Adverse means unfavorable; averse means opposed.

appraise, apprise

Appraise means to set a monetary value on; apprise means to inform.

USE THE RIGHT WORD.

I apprised him that he might get a surprise when we appraised his home.

between, among

Between is used when only two elements are involved. Usually, when more than two persons or things are involved, use among. Sometimes, if each is considered individually in relation to all the others, use between for more than two.

An agreement was reached between France, Britain and Belgium.

bi, semi

Bi means every two, as in bimonthly: every two months. Semi means half, as in semimonthly: twice a month. (Note that hyphens are not used with these prefixes.)

complement, compliment

Complement as a verb means to complete, make whole, bring to perfection; as a noun, that which completes. Compliment (verb or noun) means praise.

comprise

To embrace, contain or include. The usage "is comprised of" is incorrect.

convince, persuade

To convince is to win over by argument. Convince takes *that*, never *to*.

The counsel convinced the committee that the investigation should proceed.

To persuade is to win over by appeal to reason or feeling, usually causing a shift from one position to another. Persuade may take *to* or *that* or *of*.

The counsel persuaded the committee to continue the investigation.

disinterested, uninterested

Disinterested means impartial. Uninterested means not interested in.

effect, affect

Effect as a noun means result; as a verb, to bring about, to accomplish.

The effect of the price rise was catastrophic.

The measure effected in two days what would normally take a week.

Affect is a verb, meaning to influence.

Prices were severely affected by the ruling.

e.g., i.e.

E.g. (from the Latin *exempli gratia*) means for example.

We saw many wildflowers, e.g., trilliums, violets and monkeyflower.

I.e. (from the Latin *id est*) means that is, and explains or clarifies what preceded it.

He was a rebel without a cause, i.e., a man at war with society without knowing why.

farther, further

> Farther refers to physical distance.
>
> The farther I walked, the more my feet hurt.
>
> Further refers to degree or extent — i.e., everything except actual distance.
>
> The argument went further into the metaphysical than most people could follow.

flaunt, flout

> Flaunt means to make a boastful or ostentatious display.
>
> He flaunted his new-found wealth at every opportunity.
>
> Flout means to scoff at or treat with contempt.
>
> Those who flout the laws are called scofflaws.

infer, imply

> These two are absolutely not interchangeable. To imply is to suggest or indicate indirectly.
>
> He implied that I lacked courage.
>
> To infer is to deduce from evidence at hand.
>
> From what they were told, they inferred that the man was mentally incompetent.

ingenious, ingenuous

> Ingenious means clever, resourceful. Ingenuous means naive, innocent.

irregardless.

>   A bad word, a nonword. The one you want is regardless.

lay, lie

>   Lay is a transitive verb (takes an object).

>   All stood waiting until the hen should lay an egg.

>   Please lay the book on the table.

>   The present, past and past participle: lay, laid, laid.

>   Lie is intransitive (does not take an object).

>   Lie down, and rest.

>   The present, past and past participle: lie, lay, lain.

less, fewer

>   Less refers to quantity.

>   There's less butterfat in 2 percent milk than in whole milk.

>   Fewer refers to number.

>   Skim milk has fewer calories than whole milk.

literally, figuratively

>   Literally means actually, truly.

>   He was so angry he was literally red in the face.

>   Figuratively means metaphorically, not actually.

>   Dispute her, and she will figuratively mow you down with verbal bullets.

nauseated, nauseous

> Nauseated means seasick or sick to the stomach, and describes a person's feeling.

> The ship rolled so much that she was nauseated.

> Nauseous means causing nausea, sickening.

> The stench was nauseous.

> Don't say "I'm nauseous" unless you mean you are making those around you feel sick.

principal, principle

> Principal as an adjective means foremost, leading; as a noun, the leader or top person, as in school administration.

> Just remember that the principal is your pal.

> Principle is a noun, meaning a rule or standard.

> The founding fathers held these principles to be self-evident.

transpire

> Transpire means to leak out or become known (originally, to be emitted as a vapor). It does not mean to happen.

BE GRAMMATICAL.

Like usage (that is, using the right word), grammar is a dividing line between the writer who cares and the one who doesn't. If you want what you are writing to be as correct as it can be, you will learn and follow the fundamental rules of grammar. You need not learn everything by heart; if in doubt, look it up in one of the many complete texts, such as Hacker (see bibliography). But if you have most of the basics firmly in mind, you will save time as you write or edit.

Section II of this book gives guidelines for some of the most bothersome grammatical questions, such as agreement (verb with noun, pronoun with antecedent) and how to banish that dread interloper, the dangling participle.

Here are a few additional pointers, which can make your writing and editing less worrisome.

1. You may end a sentence with a preposition, if it reads better that way. Here are two examples of the trouble that can result from following the old "Don't end a sentence with a preposition" rule.

The first (in various versions) is ascribed to Winston Churchill, one of the masters of the English language, whose secretary kept rewriting him to remove prepositions at the end of the sentence. Churchill responded angrily:

> This is the kind of petty interference up with which I will not put!

Theodore Bernstein, in his "Dos, Don'ts and Maybes of English Usage" gives this example of awkward sentences that result from following the old rule.

> The people who insist on the rule do not always know about what they are talking. They do not know for what rules are. And it makes one wonder to what they are up.

2. It's also permitted, nowadays, to split an infinitive, if clarity is improved.

Examples:

> He promised quickly to solve the problem. (Ambiguous.)

Two better constructions (depending on what is meant):

He promised to quickly solve the problem.

He quickly promised to solve the problem.

3. Don't be afraid of "I" and "me." Many writers seem shy of using the first person, and through confusion fall into error or poor usage. Instead of "I" they will frequently use "myself."

Example:

Wrong: Joan and myself shared an office.

Better: Joan and I shared an office.

4. If the pronoun is the object of a verb or a preposition, it should always be in the objective case: me, him, her, us or them.

Example:

> Wrong: Between you and I, the rumor is
> that she left her husband yesterday.
>
> Right: Between you and me, the rumor is
> that she left her husband yesterday.

5. Conversely, the objective case of a pronoun should never be used for the subject.

Example:

> Wrong: I and her have promised to go.
>
> Right: I and she (or she and I) have
> promised to go.

PART II

ELEVEN WAYS TO IMPROVE YOUR STYLE

There are two kinds of style in writing: the first refers to the writer's distinctive mode of expressing thought in language. Thus, we say Hemingway's style was terse, Thomas Wolfe's was digressive.

The second meaning of style, and that used for this book, covers the accepted ways of handling the "mechanics" of writing, such as spelling, capitalization, punctuation and grammatical construction. The 10 chapters that follow answer the most frequently asked questions about correct style in this sense.

In many cases these rules are arbitrary, because authorities may differ, especially in punctuation. There may not always be one absolutely "right" style. But they represent the practices observed by most of the best editors and reference books today.

If you follow these rules consistently, you may not be in agreement with other authorities, but you will not be wrong. It is up to you to make your own choices — and stay with them.

Finally, the last chapter lists useful references where you will find further guidance.

1

SPELLING

There are two ways to be a good speller. One, pick the right teacher in grade school. If your teacher was strict and persistent, chances are you learned how to spell the most often misspelled words. Most of what you learned then has very likely stayed with you.

Two, if you weren't that lucky, you can still improve your spelling if you work at it. Make a list of the words you have the most trouble with, and keep it handy. For a starter, see the list below, "20 commonly misspelled words."

And take time to look words up in the dictionary if you are in doubt.

Beyond that, there are a few rules that will help.

1. The good old "i before e" rule is still valid:

    "I before e, except after c,

    or when sounded like a

    as in neighbor and weigh."

There are a few exceptions, which you will need to memorize, such as seize, weird.

Many other spelling problems have to do with suffixes.

2. When you add a suffix beginning with a consonant to a word ending in silent *e*, retain the *e*.

Examples:

awe, awesome

hate, hateful

move, movement

3. When you add a suffix beginning with a vowel to a word ending in silent *e*, you usually omit the *e*.

Examples:

hate, hater

move, movable (though moveable is a second choice)

change, changing

But there are exceptions, e.g., changeable — because spelling it as changable would alter the pronunciation.

4. When you add a suffix beginning with a vowel to an accented syllable, double the consonant.

Examples:

control, controller

occur, occurrence

prefer, preferred

compel, compelling

bag, baggage

5. When you add a suffix to a non-accented syllable, do not double the final consonant.

Examples:

bias, biased

cancel, canceling

transfer, transferee

6. For the suffixes *ible* and *able*, there are no inviolable rules. Look them up. However, if you know Latin roots, this rule sometimes helps:

   If the Latin verb ends in *are*, the suffix is *able*. If not, the suffix is *ible*.

   Examples:

   > dependable (from dependare)
   >
   > mutable (from mutare)
   >
   > collectible (from collegire)
   >
   > digestible (from digerere)

7. -ceed, -sede, -cede: these suffixes are tricky, but here's the secret of spelling words containing them.

   -ceed: only three words in the English language end in *ceed*: exceed, succeed and proceed.

   -sede: only one word ends in *sede*: supersede.

   -cede: all others end in *cede*: accede, antecede, precede, etc.

8. If you can memorize the correct spelling of these words, you will avoid the most common errors.

20 COMMONLY MISSPELLED WORDS

a lot

all right

accommodate

anoint

barbecue

boundary

consensus

defendant

definitely

dependent

embarrass

goodbye

harass

in memoriam

inoculate

memento

parallel

sacrilegious

skillful

vacuum

PUNCTUATION

COMMA

The main purpose of the comma is to show the reader where to pause. Say your sentence out loud. If it flows well without a pause, don't interrupt the flow. The trend today is to fewer commas, and many of the old rules may be broken.

Another purpose is to avoid confusion in the mind of the reader.

In many cases you may use your own judgment and instinct, but a few rules should be followed.

1. Use the comma after an introductory phrase or clause, but you may omit it if the introductory material is short.

Examples:

> While I was studying tomorrow's lesson, my elbow began to pain me.
>
> While I was studying I felt a sharp pain.
>
> Wrong: While I was studying my elbow began to hurt. (Comma needed after studying to avoid confusion.)

2. Do not use the comma between subject and verb.

   Example:

> Wrong: Diligence in learning the proper use of punctuation marks such as the comma, is sure to make you a better writer.

3. Do not use the comma between verb and object.

   Example:

> Wrong: Hartsville, located approximately two miles from the inn, offers, museums, art galleries and historic buildings.

4. It is always correct to use the comma between independent clauses joined by a coordinating conjunction, such as *and*, *but*, *or*, *nor*, *for*, *yet*, *so*. But in short sentences where there is no possibility of misreading, the comma may be omitted. The following are correct, but the comma could be omitted.

Examples:

> The dog came in, and the cat went out.
>
> The dog came in, so the cat went out.
>
> He'll pay up, or I'll know the reason why.

5. But if there could be confusion without the comma, use it.

Example:

> Wrong: Behind the garage she saw old wrecked cars and policemen were standing guard. (Use a comma after *and*, or the reader might at first think the policemen were wrecked.)

6. Use the comma in a series to separate the units, whether they are words, phrases or clauses. Use of the serial comma — that is, a comma before the last item in a series — is optional, but be consistent. Always use the serial comma if it is needed for clarity.

    Examples:

    > We ate hamburgers, cole slaw and fries. (no serial comma)
    >
    > We ate hamburgers, cole slaw, and fries. (serial comma)
    >
    > The recipe calls for lemon juice, olive oil, minced garlic, and shrimp. (Serial comma needed for clarity — otherwise reader may think shrimp is minced.)
    >
    > Wrong: We went up the trail, the trail entered the woods and the river soon appeared. (Without a comma after woods, the reader is momentarily confused into thinking the trail entered the river.)

7. Do not use the comma before a parenthesis.

Example:

> Wrong: Autumn foliage, (which is most
> colorful in New England) is best viewed in
> October.

COLON

1. Use the colon to introduce a list if the list is preceded by an independent clause.

    Examples:

    > We may choose from several destinations:
    > Vancouver, Victoria, Banff or Edmonton.
    >
    > Wrong: The possible destinations are:
    > Vancouver, Victoria, Banff and Edmonton.
    > (List not introduced by independent clause.)

2. Use the colon between independent clauses if the second clause explains or amplifies the first. In such cases, the second clause may begin with a capital or a lowercase letter, but be consistent.

Example:

> Jane is an unfortunate person: she has no
> sense of smell.

SEMICOLON

1. Use a semicolon (never a comma) between independent clauses if no conjunction is used.

   Example:

   > The night seemed endless; we thought
   > dawn would never come.

2. Use a semicolon to separate all items in a series, if some of the items have commas or other internal punctuation.

   Example:

   > The ingredients included strawberries, with
   > stems removed; Whidbeys Liqueur (or
   > other fruit liqueur); a whiff — amount is
   > optional — of ginger; and frozen orange
   > juice.

QUOTATION MARKS

1. The period and the comma always go inside the quotation mark.

    Examples:

    > "How do I love thee? Let me count the ways," wrote the poet.
    >
    > Most people believe that Shakespeare wrote "Macbeth."

2. The colon and semicolon go outside the quotation mark.

    Examples:

    > Carver drew on his own life in his story "Where I'm Calling From"; this adds to the poignancy.
    >
    > We'll choose from several destinations for our "Canadian Adventure Tour": Vancouver, Victoria, Banff and Edmonton.

3. Other punctuation goes inside or outside, depending on whether the punctuation refers to the sentence as a whole, or only to the quoted words.

Examples:

> Did he say, "The time has come"?
>
> Suddenly they exclaimed: "The time has come!"

DASH

The dash prepares the reader for a change in thought, or for an amplification. But do not use it too often. Sometimes a comma will do just as well. Never use a comma with the dash.

Example:

> Wrong: The works of art were classified by period — medieval, Renaissance or modern — , before being displayed.

PARENTHESES

If your writing is sprinkled with too many parentheses and dashes, it's a sure sign of too many afterthoughts. Go back and revise; incorporate some of the material into your sentence.

Example:

> Wrong: The first time Constance saw Paris (which was long before she met Michel, her future husband), she was taken there by Robert (the Englishman she met at Heathrow) and his cousin — a retired colonel called Orthway.
>
> Better: Constance first saw Paris when Robert and Colonel Orthway, his cousin, took her there. She'd met Robert at Heathrow. This was long before she met Michel, who would become her husband.

ELLIPSIS

The ellipsis (three dots) should be used only when you wish to indicate that you have left something out of a quotation. It is lazy to use it to finish or interrupt a sentence because you have run out of steam.

Examples:

> "The unemployment picture is much less serious now," said the President, "although the figures for February... are not yet in."

> Wrong: This hotel has everything: hot tubs, pools, terraces with every room, a marvelous view... come see for yourself!

APOSTROPHE

1. Use the apostrophe in contractions, to indicate a missing letter.

   Examples:

   > Wasn't it divine?
   >
   > It's too soon to tell.

2. Never use the apostrophe plus *s* with nouns that are not possessive in the mistaken belief that you are creating the plural.

   Example:

   > Wrong: We knew we had arrived when we saw the mailbox reading "The Robinson's."

3. Do not use the apostrophe plus *s* to make the plurals of "words as words" or of dates.

Examples:

Wrong: The report had too many "maybe's" to be useful.

Right: The report had too many "maybes" to be useful.

Wrong: It happened in the 1890's.

Right: It happened in the 1890s.

(However, such publications as The New York Times do not follow this rule. Again, choose your authority, and be consistent.)

For other guidelines on use of the apostrophe, see Possessives, Chapter 3.

POSSESSIVES

It's too bad that the English language calls for the apostrophe to form the possessive. It means we need fewer words than in French or Spanish, for example, but it also gives us more opportunity for mistakes. Still, for the time being we must go with the customary and accepted usage. These are the basic rules, followed by most writers. (But not all. See sections on possessives in Judd and the "Chicago Manual of Style.")

1. For singular common nouns, no matter what the final consonant, and for singular proper nouns not ending in *s*: use apostrophe and *s*.

Examples:

> the lad's sister
>
> the dance's steps
>
> the bus's exhaust
>
> Ted's bat

2. For singular proper nouns ending in *s*: use the apostrophe only.

Examples:

> Ted Williams' bat
>
> James' pipe
>
> Achilles' heel
>
> Kansas' corn

3. For plural nouns ending in *s*, whether common or proper: use the apostrophe only.

Examples:

> the Maritime Provinces' boundaries
>
> the students' books
>
> states' rights
>
> the Joneses' front yard

Note that the plural of Jones is Joneses. The rule for plurals: if the noun ends with *s*, *ss*, *ch*, *sh*, *x* or *z*, add *es*. This may result in some awkward-looking possessives. Nevertheless, these are correct.

Examples:

> the Hendrixes' tickets
>
> the churches' pastors
>
> the masses' revolt
>
> the Bushes' family

4. For plural nouns not ending in *s*: use apostrophe and *s*.

    Examples:

    > women's rights
    >
    > the alumni's delegates
    >
    > the men's room

5. For these possessive pronouns, never use the apostrophe:
    hers, theirs, yours, ours, its.

    Examples:

    > The book was hers, though I thought it was
    > yours.
    >
    > Ours not to reason why.
    >
    > The responsibility is theirs.
    >
    > Death has lost its sting.

6. The most important rule of all: When using "its," determine if it is a possessive or a contraction. The possessive never takes the apostrophe; the contraction always does.

Examples:

> Honesty has its rewards. (possessive)
>
> It's true. (contraction)
>
> It's too bad, but the dog has lost its bone.

DANGLERS

This is the rule: A participle, participial phrase or modifying phrase at the beginning of a sentence must modify the subject of the sentence (or the subject of the following clause, if there is one).

Some definitions: A participle is a form of a verb usually ending in, *ing*, e.g., running, looking, being. Or it may be a past participle ending in *ed*, such as exhausted, worried.

A participial phrase is the phrase that includes the participle, e.g., running to work, looking to the future, being hospitable.

Other modifying phrases may be formed with prepositions, e.g., after a decade of being a glamour drug.

In the battle against dangling modifiers, the important thing to look for is a phrase or word at the beginning of a sentence that does not apply to what immediately follows it. It is usually easy to rewrite the sentence to make it grammatically correct. Here are some examples of sentences with danglers, and how they were repaired.

Examples:

Wrong: Running to work, a dog chased me half a block. (This implies that the dog was running to work.)

Better: When I was running to work, a dog chased me half a block.

Wrong: Looking out the window, two birds came into her view. (The birds were not looking out the window.)

Better: As she looked out the window, two birds came into her view.

Wrong: Being of a hospitable nature, my door is always open. (Is my door of a hospitable nature?)

Better: Being of a hospitable nature, I always keep my door open.

Wrong: Exhausted by two nights without sleep, my bed looked very good to me. (Implication: the bed had not slept for two nights.)

Better: I was exhausted by two nights without sleep, and my bed looked very good to me.

Worried about civil unrest, 20 of the protesters were rounded up by order of the police. (The protesters were not the ones worried about civil unrest.)

Better: The police, worried about civil unrest, rounded up 20 of the protesters.

Wrong: After decades of being a glamour drug, researchers are starting to uncover the truth about cocaine. (The researchers were not a glamour drug, cocaine was.)

Better: Researchers are starting to uncover the truth about cocaine, which has been a glamour drug for decades.

Sometimes the dangling modifier is merely amusing, but sometimes it is confusing.

Examples:

Wrong: Having recovered from pneumonia, his mother took him abroad. (Did he recover from pneumonia, or did his mother?)

Better: When he had recovered from pneumonia, his mother took him abroad.

Or: When his mother had recovered from pneumonia, she took him abroad.

PRONOUNS

Pronouns — words that take the place of a noun — can cause confusion in the writer's mind in a couple of areas:

Should you use the nominative (subject) case or the objective?

Should you use a singular or plural verb?

1. Subject or object?

The rule: Pronouns used as subjects of a verb should always be in the nominative case; pronouns used as objects of a verb or preposition should be in the objective case.

NOMINATIVE	OBJECTIVE
I	me
you	you
he	him
she	her
we	us
they	them

A frequent problem with pronouns arises when the object is two or more people.

Examples:

> Wrong: The letter was addressed to both Uncle John and I.
>
> Right: The letter was addressed to both Uncle John and me.

Sometimes it is hard to find the real subject of the sentence, and therefore to know whether to use the nominative or objective pronoun. It may help to rewrite the sentence.

Examples:

> Wrong: To eat that entire pie there were only you and me. (Turn the sentence around, and you will see that the subject is you and I.)
>
> Right: Only you and I were there to eat that entire pie.
>
> Wrong: The author, we later learned, was her.

Right: We later learned that the author was she.

Or: We later learned that she was the author.

Sometimes the verb is understood.

Examples:

Wrong: Is she as old as him?

Right: Is she as old as he (is)?

Wrong: No one is in more danger than him.

Right: No one is in more danger than he (is).

Who and *whom* are no problem if you remember that *who* must be the subject of a verb and *whom* must be the object of a verb or preposition.

Examples:

Wrong: Who will the investigating committee call on next?

> Right: Whom will the investigating committee call on next?

Before using *whom* make sure it isn't really a relative pronoun used as a subject of a following verb.

Examples:

> Wrong: He is a person whom I think is well qualified.
>
> Right: He is a person who I think is well qualified. (Remove "I think" and it is clear that *who* must be the subject of "is well qualified.")

This also applies to *whoever* and *whomever*.

Examples:

> Wrong: He'd sell the paintings to whomever had the wherewithal.
>
> Right: He'd sell the paintings to whoever had the wherewithal. (*Whoever* is the subject of the verb "had.")

Wrong: You may sell them to whoever you like.

Right: You may sell them to whomever you like. (*Whomever* is the object of "like.")

2. Singular or plural verb?

This question arises most often with indefinite pronouns like these. They always take a singular verb.

each

every

either

neither

anyone

anybody

everyone

everybody

someone

somebody

no one

nobody

Examples:

> Each — whether fish, flesh or fowl — has its purpose.
>
> Every avenue and solution is being examined.
>
> Is either of the answers the correct one?
>
> Neither of the two answers is correct.
>
> Anyone in his right mind knows that.
>
> Or, to avoid the charge of sexism: Any sensible person knows that.
>
> Everyone who wants to be saved is required to step forward.
>
> Everybody who came to the meeting wants to speak.
>
> No one but the conductor and the orchestra knows what the encore will be.

AGREEMENT

It sounds simple, and sometimes it is. The rule: the verb must agree in number with its subject, the pronoun with its antecedent. Some pointers to help you catch disagreements.

1. Don't be confused by words that intervene between subject and verb.

   Example:

   > The complexity of the educational system — its teachers and students, its classrooms and playing fields, its pencils and computer terminals — is daunting.

2. Even if other words are connected to the subject by *together with*, *as well as*, *in addition to* or *including*, use a singular verb.

Examples:

> The President, together with his entire party, plans a weekend at Camp David.
>
> Her taste in clothes, in addition to her sensitivity to perfume, is impeccable.
>
> The frog, as well as the toad and the newt, is equally at home in water or on land.
>
> The company's product line, including trucks, pickups, tractors and all spare parts, is up for review.

3. Having decided whether to treat a collective noun as a singular or plural, make sure all verbs and related pronouns are in agreement. If awkwardness results, rewrite.

Examples:

> Wrong: Boeing is best known as an airplane manufacturer, but they make a lot of other things too.

Better: Boeing is best known as an airplane manufacturer, but the company makes a lot of other things too.

Wrong: The committee was ushered into the room, where they began their deliberations.

Better: The committee was ushered into the room, where the members began their deliberations.

4. When the elements of a compound subject are connected by *or* or *nor*, the verb should agree with the nearer element.

Examples:

Either the figures were wrong or the arithmetic was.

Neither the figures nor the arithmetic was wrong.

Neither the arithmetic nor the figures were wrong.

7

PARALLELISM

This simply means that if the parts of a sentence are "parallel" or comparable, they should have the same grammatical structure. If you have two or more words, phrases or clauses that serve the same purpose in your sentence, express them all in the same form. Non-parallel sentence segments are not necessarily ungrammatical; but they are a barrier to the reader's comprehension and make for choppy writing.

Examples:

Wrong: For the would-be writer, the road to professionalism has three requirements: constant practice, using good reference books and never to be afraid of revising.

Better: For the would-be writer, the road to professionalism has three requirements: constant practice, use of good reference books and a willingness to revise. (The sentence reads more smoothly if all three requirements are nouns.)

Wrong: I was sure of getting a good recommendation and that I would be offered the job.

Better: I was sure that I would get a good recommendation and that I would be offered the job.

Wrong: Neither a borrower nor a person who lends money be.

Better: Neither a borrower nor a lender be.

Wrong: The marketing plan has many advantages, such as increasing consumer awareness, to build sales, and money-saving potential.

Better: The marketing plan has many advantages, such as increasing consumer awareness, building sales, and saving money.

ABBREVIATIONS

Because there are many customs and styles for abbreviations, the most important thing to look for is consistency. Refer to the same good stylebook whenever in doubt about abbreviations, and you will not go wrong. The Associated Press "Stylebook," the "Chicago Manual of Style" and "Words into Type" are all dependable.

Here are a few pointers on how to use abbreviations.

1. To spell out, or not? Some well-known abbreviations are easily recognized and need not be spelled out. They take no periods.

Examples:

CIA, USSR, FDR, NBC, YWCA, NFL, TWA, OPEC.

But if you doubt the reader's familiarity with the abbreviation, don't use it just to save a little space. Spell out the words.

It is helpful to the reader to identify the abbreviation (if it is not a commonplace one) the first time you use it, if you plan to keep using it. This may be in either of these two ways:

> The Arts & Entertainment network (A&E) offers a wide range of programs.
>
> A&E (the Arts & Entertainment network) offers a wide range of programs.

But if the name is not at all well known and the abbreviation might be confusing on the second use, or if the second use comes far after the first use, continue to use the full name or a shortened version.

Examples:

> Wrong: The International Association of Collectors of James Dean Memorabilia (IACJDM) met yesterday in Long Beach. After a full day of conferences and exhibits, the IACJDM members adjourned to the hotel banquet room for a joint meeting with the Marilyn Monroe Memorial Society (MMMS). Later, the IACJDM and the MMMS members all attended a reception at the Film Personality Museum (FPM).

Better: The International Association of Collectors of James Dean Memorabilia met yesterday in Long Beach. After a full day of conferences and exhibits, the James Dean group adjourned to the hotel banquet room for a joint meeting with the Marilyn Monroe Memorial Society. Later, both the James Dean and Marilyn Monroe organizations attended a reception at the Film Personality Museum.

2. Academic degrees should be abbreviated after the name, and set off with a comma. Note that there is no space between the abbreviations.

Examples:

The main speaker was Howard Harris, Ph.D.

We celebrate the graduation of Patricia Horsley, M.A.

3. Titles: abbreviate these if used directly before a full proper name; but if used before the surname alone, spell out: Gov., Lt. Gov., Dr., Rep., Sen., Sgt., Lt., Capt., Col., Gen., Prof.

Examples:

> Gov. Mario Cuomo stated his opinions on
> the death penalty.
>
> Governor Cuomo stated his views.

4. Junior and senior: abbreviate, with caps and with a period, and set off with commas, after the full name.

Examples:

> Mrs. Martin Luther King, Sr., was
> mentioned.
>
> During Act II, Sammy Davis, Jr., performed.

5. Days of the week should be spelled out in text, but may be abbreviated in tabulations.

Examples:

> There will be a full moon on Tuesday,
> Aug. 22.

> (Headings for a table): Sun., Mon., Tues., Wed., Thurs., Fri., Sat.

6. Months are abbreviated when used with a specific date, but spelled out when used alone.

Examples:

> The date is Sept. 22.
>
> The date is sometime in September.

7. Time of day (a.m., p.m.) is usually lowercase, though some style manuals prefer caps. In either case, always use periods; and never use a.m. or p.m. with morning or afternoon.

Examples:

> Wrong: The bomb fell at 7:13 a.m. this morning.
>
> Better: The bomb fell at 7:13 a.m., or at 7:13 this morning.

8.   A.D., B.C.: A.D. precedes the date, B.C. follows it. Nowadays, especially in scientific writing, you may see B.P. (Before the Present) instead of B.C. (Before Christ). Do not use spaces between these abbreviations.

Examples:

In A.D. 711, the Muslims overran Spain.

Julius Caesar invaded Britain in 54 B.C.

The last Ice Age was about 10,000 B.P.

WHO, WHICH OR THAT?

1. Use *who* for persons, or for animals with names.

    Examples:

    > The one who was defeated will appeal.
    >
    > My cat Tiger, whom I dearly loved, has run away.

2. Use *which* for things and unnamed animals.

Examples:

> The report, which I wrote in an hour, was two pages.
>
> The fox, which had been nearly tamed, reverted to the wild.

3. Use *that* for animals and things, and sometimes for persons.

Examples:

> Chickens that try to cross the road don't always make it.
>
> Boats that are under 30 feet long are in another class .
>
> The only person that could answer the question is in Tibet.

4. To introduce a clause, either *which* or *that* may be used, but not interchangeably. Here is the general rule:

If a comma can be inserted, use *which*. But if the information is essential to the meaning, use *that* and no comma.

See the above sentence, "The report, which I wrote in an hour, was two pages." The words "which I wrote in an hour" give additional information about the report but are not essential to the meaning of the sentence. They do not restrict the meaning. So they are set off by commas, or by parentheses. Hence the terms: parenthetical, nonrestrictive or nonessential clause.

But in the sentence, "The report that I wrote was 22 pages long," the words "that I wrote" are essential to distinguish this report from all other reports. They define, identify and restrict the antecedent noun, report. Hence the terms: restrictive or essential clause.

QUOTATIONS

See the "Punctuation" section of this book (Part II, Chapter 2) for use of quotation marks with other punctuation.

These are the general rules for when to use quotation marks.

1.   Use quotation marks to set aside quoted material: dialogue, fragments of poetry or prose, words used as words and unfamiliar words.

Examples:

"Will you lend me your steed?" asked the king. "Never!" replied his equerry.

> When Robert Frost wrote, "Good fences make good neighbors," he was quoting his neighbor.
>
> As Joseph Conrad observed in "Lord Jim," "Vanity plays lurid tricks with our memory."
>
> The word "masterful" is often used when what is really meant is "masterly."
>
> For those not familiar with music, we should explain that "segue" means to proceed without interruption.

2. Use quotation marks around titles of these works:

books

movies

operas

plays

poems

short stories, essays

songs

television programs

lectures, speeches

works of art

Examples:

The title of Thomas Wolfe's "You Can't Go
Home Again" has been quoted by many
people who have not read the book.

How many times have you seen "Batman"?

Verdi's "La Traviata" has been a vehicle for
some of the world's leading sopranos.

How closely does Shakespeare's "Richard
the Second," one of his historical plays,
actually follow history?

Keats' "Ode to a Grecian Urn" is a poem
that lingers in the memory.

Imagine hearing, for the first time, the
Beatles' "Strawberry Fields Forever" !

The high ratings of "The Cosby Show"
continued, year in and year out.

Shirley Jackson's story "The Lottery"
brought thousands of letters to The New
Yorker.

For an evocative tribute to a beloved car,
read E. B. White's "Farewell, My Lovely!"

It was a stirring speech, now known as
Lincoln's "Gettysburg Address."

> The class is required to visit the Louvre to see the statue "The Winged Victory of Samothrace" and the painting "Mona Lisa" by Leonardo da Vinci.

You will find that some stylebooks recommend italics rather than quotes for book titles. You may decide what style to use, then stick to it.

Also, note that the name of a publication (e.g., The New Yorker) is not placed in quotes, or italicized. The same would be true for the name of a newspaper. This follows the practice of the AP "Stylebook," but other authorities may differ. Again, choose your own course, and be consistent.

BIBLIOGRAPHY OF USEFUL REFERENCES

You will, of course have a good dictionary handy, and perhaps a spelling guide. And your word processor probably has a spelling checker. But in addition, the books on this brief list will be a comfort and a help, as you write and edit.

The Associated Press. "Stylebook and Libel Manual."

Bernstein, Theodore. "Dos, Don'ts & Maybes of English Usage." Also by this author: "Watch Your Language" and "The Careful Writer."

Fowler, H.W. "A Dictionary of Modern English Usage," revised by Sir Ernest Gowers.

Hacker, Diana. "Rules for Writers."

Judd, Karen. "Copyediting: A Practical Guide."

BIBLIOGRAPHY OF USEFUL REFERENCES

Ross-Larson, Bruce. "Edit Yourself."

Skillin, Marjorie and Robert Gay. "Words into Type."

Strunk, William and E. B. White. "The Elements of Style."

University of Chicago. "The Chicago Manual of Style."

PART III

EDITING AND PROOFREADING SYMBOLS

The same symbols, for the most part, are used for copyediting and proofreading. The difference is that in copyediting, the corrections are made at the point of the mistake (since most copy is double-spaced, this is easy); whereas in proofreading of copy already set in type, corrections are made in the margin, with a mark at the point of the mistake.

These are the commonly used symbols.

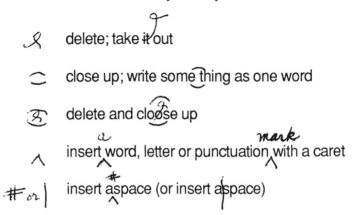

delete; take it out

close up; write some thing as one word

delete and close up

insert word, letter or punctuation with a caret

insert a space (or insert a space)

⁋	new paragraph
stet	let it stand ~~as written~~
↻	trasnpose; the change order
sp	spell out an (abbrev.) or a figure, as (300)
≡	set in capital letters
/	set in Lowercase letters
ital	set in italic
bf	set in boldface
⩗	insert apostrophe
⌃	insert comma
⊙	insert period
⊚	change a comma to a period
⦂	insert colon
= ⌃	insert hyphen
⩔ ⩔	insert quotation marks
run in	run in with preceding words
⌐	start a new line

This shows how copyediting marks are used.

The cost of housing, medical care, insurance, utilities, and other essentials continue to escalate. For low income families, these needs may take presedence in deciding how scarce resources are to be spent. The result is that they have less food on the table, and it is less nutritious. Srs. on fixed incomes are particularly vulnerable.

Lack of housing — e.g., homelessness — is the most vivid and visible symptom of poverty, especially in cities and urban areas. The site of the homeless sleeping in the street next to costly high rise buildings is distressingly frequent. There seems to be little doubt that inordinately high housing costs are part of the cause. The Cencus Bureau reports that the majority of renters with incomes below $7,000 dollars spent 60% of their income on rent and utilities in 1983. Even if they could afford low cost housing many stet families can not find it. In one major city, fifteen thousand low cost housing units have been lost since the 1960s; and urban neighborhoods are being rebuilt for higher income residents. This forces low income residents to move, often to suburbs far from their jobs, or depend on shelters. In this city, thirty percent of shelter residents are working people, who have been unable to find afordable housing.

Adding to the problem is the overcrowding in shelters, which simply can not accomodate all those who wish simply to lay down and rest.

Now, the same passage, after correction.

The cost of housing, medical care, insurance, utilities and other essentials continues to escalate. For low-income families, these needs may take precedence in deciding how to spend scarce resources. As a result, they have less food on the table, and it is less nutritious. Seniors on fixed incomes are particularly vulnerable.

Lack of housing — i.e., homelessness — is the most vivid and visible symptom of poverty, especially in cities and urban areas. The sight of the homeless sleeping in the street next to costly high-rise buildings is distressingly frequent. High housing costs are part of the cause. The Census Bureau reports that the majority of renters with incomes below $7,000 spent 60 percent of their income on rent and utilities in 1983.

Even if they could afford low-cost housing, many families cannot find it. In one major city, 15,000 low-cost housing units have been lost since the 1960s; and urban neighborhoods are being rebuilt for higher-income residents. This forces low-income residents to move, often to suburbs far from their jobs, or to depend on shelters. In this city, 30 percent of shelter residents are working people, who have been unable to find affordable housing.

Adding to the problem is the overcrowding in shelters.

An example of a portion of the same copy, with proofreading marks, follows. Note that corrections may be made in either margin. If more than one correction occurs in the same line, separate with diagonals.

The cost of housing,

medical care, insurance,

utilities/ and other esentials

continue to escalate. For low

income families, these needs

may take presedence in

deciding how scarce resources to spend

del   are to be spent. The result

del   is that they have less food

on the table, and it is less

nutritious. Srs on fixed   sp

incomes are particularly

vulberable.

INDEX

NOTES

NOTES

NOTES

There are three errors in "Editing Guide." See if you can find them.

The text portion of "Editing Guide" is set in twelve point TimesTen Roman™, a typeface specially created by Adobe Systems Inc.® for easily readable textbooks.

Typeset by Blue Zoo, formerly BOSS Enterprises, Tacoma, Washington.